TABLE OF CONTENTS

025

MY HERO ACADEMIA
BY KOHEI HORIKOSHI

002

ONE-PUNCH MAN
STORY BY ONE
ART BY YUSUKE MURATA

052

YU-GI-OH! ARC-V
ORIGINAL CONCEPT BY KAZUKI TAKAHASHI
PRODUCTION SUPPORT: STUDIO DICE
STORY BY SHIN YOSHIDA, ART BY NAOHITO MIYOSHI
DUEL COMPOSITION: MASAHIRO HIKOKUBO

BLACK CLOVER
BY YŪKI TABATA

0

JUMP PACK SPRIN 201

?!

THOOM...

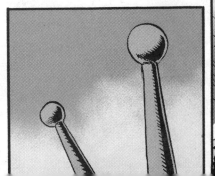

RRMMMMMMMMM

THE EXPLOSIONS ROCKING **CITY A** HAVE SPREAD, BLANKETING THE WHOLE...

THE RUMBLING AND TREMORS CONTINUE!!

15:20

CONGESTION / LINES A AND B SHUT DOWN BOTH WAYS

...

HERE I GO...

9

I EXIST BECAUSE OF HUMANKIND'S CONSTANT POLLUTION OF THE ENVIRONMENT!

I AM VAC-CINE MAN!

AND YOU HUMANS ARE THE DISEASE-CAUSING GERMS KILLING IT!

THE EARTH IS A SINGLE LIVING ORGANISM!

KRUMBL KRUMBL

SPLAT

...

DARN IT!!!

FINISHED IN ONE PUNCH AGAIN!

TO BE CONTINUED IN VOL. 1

MY HERO ACADEMIA

BY KOHEI HORIKOSHI

Middle school student Izuku Midoriya wants to be a hero more than anything, but he hasn't got an ounce of power in him. With no chance of ever getting into the prestigious U.A. High School for budding heroes, his life is looking more and more like a dead end. Then an encounter with All Might, the greatest hero of them all, gives him a chance to change his destiny…

VOLUMES 1–2

AVAILABLE IN
PRINT AND DIGITAL
AT VIZ.COM!

HUMANS HAVE NO NEED FOR PARTS THEY DON'T USE, YOU SEE.

IT HAS TO DO WITH THE PRESENCE OR ABSENCE OF THE EXTRA JOINT IN THE PINKY TOE.

Know about this?

HOWEVER, EARLY QUIRK RESEARCH DISCOVERED ONE IMPORTANT FINDING.

...EITHER ONE OF HIS PARENTS' QUIRKS OR A COMPOSITE OF THE TWO.

BY THE AGE OF FOUR, A CHILD SHOULD MANIFEST...

AND THOSE WITHOUT THE JOINT REPRESENT THE NEXT STAGE OF EVOLUTION.

IT'S BECOMING QUITE RARE NOWADAYS, BUT...

HE POSSESSES *NO* QUIRK AT ALL.

IZUKU HERE HAS *TWO* JOINTS.

NO MATTER WHAT KIND OF TROUBLE YOU'RE IN...

...HE'LL SAVE YOU WITH A SMILE.

AND HE'S SMILING!!

WAHHHH

RUMBLE

MOM...

...

FSSSSSSH

A SUPER-COOL HERO LIKE THAT.

...!!

THAT'S...

...WHAT I WANNA BE.

SHUP

NO, MOM...

NO...

BACK THEN, WHAT I WANTED YOU TO SAY WAS...

I'M SORRY, IZUKU. I'M SORRY!

TO KEEP MY CHIN UP AND KEEP MOVING FORWARD!!

I DECIDED NOT TO CARE WHAT ANYONE SAYS!!

BAM!!

頭上注意 2m

THAT WAS WHEN I DECIDED.

THANK GOODNESS.

TAT

HEY... UH.

HEY!

HEY!

HEY!

SLAP SLAP SLAP SLAP

HA HA

MISTAKES LIKE THAT AREN'T MY STYLE, BUT...

...THIS IS A STRANGE LAND TO ME. AND BESIDES I'M OFF CAMERA!!

HA HA

HA HA

...FOR GETTING YOU CAUGHT UP IN MY VILLAIN HUNT.

APOLOGIES...

YOU'RE OKAY! EXCELLENT!!

WHA-?!

NO. 1 HERO: ALL MIGHT

ALL MIGHT! HE'S HERE... HE'S REALLY HERE!! UP CLOSE, I CAN REALLY SEE...

...HE'S DRAWN IN A TOTALLY DIFFERENT STYLE!!

I'VE CONTAINED THE VILLAIN!!

BROOOB!

BUT MY SUCCESS HERE IS ALL THANKS TO YOU!!

HEY, NOW!!

BA—M

AHEM.

NN...

I...NEED TO ASK YOU... SO MANY THINGS... GAH! YOU...

OKAY, OKAY. JUST DO ME A FAVOR AND CLOSE YOUR EYES AND MOUTH!

FLAP FLAP

IF I...LET GO NOW... I'LL... I'LL DIE...!

RELEASE ME! SUCH ENTHUSIASM IS A BIT MUCH!

TRUE ENOUGH!!

GRAB

FLAIL

PAUSE

PLIP

Darn!!

THAT IDIOT... IF NOT FOR HIM, I COULD'VE...

DARN IT!

FWIP

WHERE AM I?

...

WHOOSH

YEAH, YOU WENT TOO FAR TODAY.

HAVEN'T YOU KNOWN HIM SINCE YOU WERE KIDS?

IT'S HIS FAULT FOR MESSING WITH ME.

KICK

H-HEY!!

?

THOUGHT I TOLD YOU TO STOP SMOKING!!

GRRR

GET CAUGHT, AND IT'LL GO ON MY RECORD TOO...

...JUST PISSES ME OFF.

SEEING HIM SO FULL OF STUPID DREAMS LIKE WHEN WE WERE KIDS...

WHOA!

BOOM

A BODY...

...WITH A GOOD QUIRK.

HOPEFULLY THE PEOPLE DOWNSTAIRS WILL HELP US GET DOWN.

OF ALL THE...!!

GRR

I'VE NO TIME THOUGH! TRULY!!

WEEZ WEEZ

SCARY...

CRASH

...CAN I STILL BE A HERO?!

EVEN WITHOUT A QUIRK...

SH F

WAIT! UM...

NO!! I WILL NOT WAIT.

...BECOME A HERO LIKE YOU?

CAN SOMEONE WITHOUT A QUIRK...

BADUM

QUIRKS ARE...

I THINK THAT SAVING PEOPLE IS JUST ABOUT THE COOLEST THING SOMEONE CAN DO.

THAT'S WHY... MAYBE THAT'S WHY...

BUT I'VE ALWAYS BEEN PICKED ON...

BECAUSE I DON'T HAVE A QUIRK, I... WELL, MAYBE THAT'S NOT THE ONLY REASON.

OH NO... DARN IT ALL...

WHOOSH

SHF!...

I WANT TO BE THE STRONGEST HERO, JUST LIKE Y—

THE WAY YOU SAVE PEOPLE WITH THAT FEARLESS SMILE!

WHAAAAAT?!

FSSHH

...

WHOA!

I AM ALL MIGHT.

...

BLAH BLAH

YOU'RE ALL SHRIVELED UP! HUH?! WERE YOU... HUH?! A FAKE?! AN IMPOSTOR?! SO THIN!!

NO WAY!!

YOU KNOW HOW PEOPLE HOLD IN THEIR GUT AT THE POOL?

IT'S LIKE THAT!

NO WAY!!

NO WAY...

BUT DON'T WRITE ABOUT IT ON THE INTERNET, OKAY?

YOU'VE SEEN THE REAL ME, KID.

SIT

Sigh...

A FEARLESS SMILE, HUH...

EEP!

SWF

I'VE WASTED AWAY BECAUSE OF THE AFTER-EFFECTS OF THOSE SURGERIES.

MY RESPIRATORY SYSTEM WAS NEARLY DESTROYED, AND MY STOMACH WAS REMOVED.

I CAN ONLY DO MY HERO WORK FOR ABOUT THREE HOURS A DAY NOW.

FIVE YEARS AGO...AN ENEMY DID THIS TO ME.

...MUST NEVER BE DAUNTED BY EVIL.

A SYMBOL OF PEACE WHO SAVES PEOPLE WITH A SMILE...

THAT LOWLIFE? HE COULD NEVER DO THIS TO ME!

WAS THAT WHEN YOU FOUGHT TOXIC CHAINSAW?

FIVE YEARS AGO ...?

You've done your homework.

CLENCH

THAT IS, I ASKED THAT IT NOT BE MADE PUBLIC.

THIS WAS NEVER MADE PUBLIC.

WITHOUT POWER, CAN ONE BECOME A HERO? NO, I SHOULD THINK NOT.

A PRO SHOULD ALWAYS BE READY TO RISK HIS LIFE.

...IS TO STAVE OFF THE OVERWHELMING PRESSURE AND FEAR I FEEL.

THE REASON I SMILE...

BROOM

WHOA!!

ARGH!

WE NEED THAT KID TO HOLD ON JUST A BIT LONGER!

UNTIL THEN, KEEP THE DAMAGE TO A MINIMUM. SOMEONE'LL COME!

JUST GOTTA WAIT FOR SOMEONE WITH THE RIGHT QUIRK TO SHOW UP!!

NO GOOD! THERE'S NO ONE HERE WHO CAN STOP HIM!!

GRAB

THAT'S WHEN IT HAPPENED!!

WEEZ

WEEZ

IF ONLY I HAD THE POWER TO BLOW HIM AWAY!

SHOOT!

DEALING WITH THAT FAN LED TO THIS!!

I LOST TRACK OF TIME!

PA-THETIC...

THROB

PATHETIC!!

EVEN AS A THIRD-YEAR, HE STILL CAN'T FACE REALITY.

YOU NEED TO BE REALISTIC.

将来の為の ヒーロー分析 No.13

DON'T CRY! YOU KNEW ALREADY, RIGHT?!

THIS IS REALITY...

EVEN...THE BEST OF THE BEST SAID IT...

SNIFFLE

IT'S BECAUSE I KNEW...THAT I TRIED SO HARD...

IT'S TIME TO START THINKING SERIOUSLY ABOUT YOUR FUTURES!

GRABBED...? SO HE'S ENDURING THAT SAME PAIN?!

CREEP CREEP

UNBELIEVABLE...

SEEMS THE VILLAIN'S GRABBED A MIDDLE SCHOOLER.

WHY'RE THE HEROES JUST STANDING THERE?

...

...

ALL MIGHT LET HIM GO?! DID HE DROP HIM?! THAT MEANS...

...

THIS IS MY FAULT!

THEN WHAT'S ALL MIGHT DOING NOW?!

YEAH, I SAW HIM EARLIER.

!

ALL MIGHT?! NO WAY! HE'S REALLY HERE?!

ISN'T IT THE ONE ALL MIGHT WAS CHASING?

HEY, THAT VILLAIN...

!

A HERO'S BOUND TO COME...

I'M SO SORRY! SOMEONE WILL COME TO SAVE YOU SOON...

HANG IN THERE... I'M SORRY!

THIS GUY CAN'T BE CAUGHT. WE HAVE TO WAIT FOR SOMEONE WITH THE RIGHT QUIRK TO SHOW UP!

IT'S MY FAULT ALL MIGHT CAN'T DO ANYTHING!!

TO BE CONTINUED IN VOL. 1

YU-GI-OH! ARC-V

ORIGINAL CONCEPT BY KAZUKI TAKAHASHI, PRODUCTION SUPPORT BY STUDIO DICE
STORY BY SHIN YOSHIDA, ART BY NAOHITO MIYOSHI, DUEL COMPOSITION: MASAHIRO HIKOKUBO

On the mean streets of Maiami City, you've got to work hard to be the best. Yuzu Hiiragi and her father run a dueling school that's seen better days. If only they had a star teacher bring in new students! When a rogue Duelist known as Phantom appears in the city, Yuzu may have found a savior, but Phantom will have to deal with the LC Corporation's special forces before he can get into any community service!

READ THE LATEST CHAPTERS
AT SHONENJUMP.VIZ.COM!

TUMP

SNIFF

WHAT'S THE MATTER?

?

LEO CORPORATION...

...AND I DIDN'T GET TO SEE ANY REAL MONSTERS.

...AND WHEN I GOT TO THE *LEO CORPORATION DUEL TOURNAMENT,* IT WAS ALREADY OVER...

I OVER- SLEPT...

AT THE LC TOURNAMENT, THEY MAKE THE MONSTERS PHYSICAL WITH SOLID VISION.

I SEE...

I WANTED TO SEE A DRAGON *SO BAD!!*

WAAAAAH

MASS SENSORS HAVE ACTIVATED WITHIN CITY LIMITS!

BEEEEEP

EMERGENCY!

BIP

BIP

ANALYSIS CONFIRMS IT IS THE ODD-EYES PHANTOM DRAGON!!

TARGET SIGHTED!!

SWIP

ODD-EYES...

AT LAST YOU SHOW YOURSELF, PHANTOM!!

SOMEONE BELIEVED TO BE THE PHANTOM IS TRAVELING NORTH OVER THE ROOFTOPS!

...THE DESTINY FACTOR WHO HOLDS OUR FUTURE IN HIS HANDS...

THE TRUE IDENTITY OF THE PHANTOM...

ZZZT

...IS YUYA SAKAKI!!

!

FWASH

TOMP

THEY'RE CLOSING IN!

WHUP

WOO-HOO! LOOK!!

WHUP

ARE YOU ENJOYING THIS?!

WHUP

GIVE IT UP, PHANTOM!!

OR SHOULD I SAY *YUYA SAKAKI*?!

YOU'RE TRAPPED LIKE A RAT!!

DADOOM

...

AND YOUR OPPONENT...

...IS ME.

VERY WELL...

!

FLUP

...SHALL I SHOW MY FACE?

BLACK CLOVER

BY YŪKI TABATA

Asta is a young boy who dreams of becoming the greatest mage in the kingdom. Only one problem—he can't use any magic! Can someone who can't use magic really become the Wizard King? One thing's for sure—Asta will never give up!

READ THE LATEST CHAPTERS

AT SHONENJUMP.VIZ.COM!

VOLUME 1

COMING 2016!

SO FIRST, I NEED TO TRAIN MY BODY!

...

RARRGHHHぅぁぁぁぁぁぁ

つぉぉぉぁぁぁ

THIS IS SOMETHING I'LL NEVER GIVE UP ON!

I'M GOING TO BE THE WIZARD KING!

MARCH. AROUND THE TIME WHEN THE FIREFLY DANDELION FLUFFS FLOAT AROUND...

ONCE A YEAR, IN VARIOUS PLACES IN THE COUNTRY, ALL THE 15-YEAR-OLDS ARE GATHERED...

...TO HOLD AN AWARDING CEREMONY FOR GRIMOIRES. THESE GRIMOIRES INCREASE THEIR MAGICAL POWERS.

TMP

TMP

TMP

GREEEAK

I AM THE MASTER OF THIS GRIMOIRE TOWER.

HEH♪ HEH♪ HEH♪

DOES HE REALLY NEED TO GIVE THEM GRIMOIRES TOO?

BUT ONE OF THEM IS HOT.

...NOR HAVE WE HAD ONE ACHIEVE GREATNESS BY JOINING THE MAGIC KNIGHTS.

THEY LOOK SO SHABBY.

HEH!

WE HAVEN'T HAD A WIZARD KING FROM THIS AREA...

WOW, I'M A FULL-FLEDGED MAGE STARTING TODAY.

HEY, LOOK! THOSE ARE THE ORPHANS FROM THE CHURCH.

NOW, IT IS TIME FOR...

THAT'S IMPOSSIBLE.

I SINCERELY WISH THAT SOMEONE AMONG YOU WILL BECOME THE WIZARD KING.

GLARE

I'M SERIOUS HERE!

LOOK, MINE IS BIGGER.

Heh.

WHATEVER! MINE'S THICKER.

Haha!

THIS...

...IS MY GRIMOIRE!

UM...

WE'RE GOING TO TAKE THE TEST IN SIX MONTHS TO JOIN THE MAGIC KNIGHTS.

Heh.

おおっ

OOH

I'LL... THINK ABOUT MY FUTURE AFTER MY GRIMOIRE HAS MORE ENTRIES.

YES, NOW I CAN LEAVE THIS TOWN AND GO TO THE CITY!

I'M GOING TO TAKE OVER THE FAMILY BUSINESS!

...MY GRIMOIRE'S NOT COMING.

SILENCE

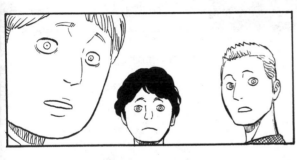

WHAAAAAAAT?!

TRY AGAIN NEXT YEAR.

SHOCK-

BUZZ

BUZZ

MURMUR

MURMUR

...

AHEM

UH
...

No way.

IT'S ACTUALLY AMAZING.

THAT'S TOO FUNNY!

WHAT THE HECK ?!

! SHOOOOOM

CHUCKLE

I GUESS IT'S WHAT YOU CAN EXPECT FROM THE SLUMS. I DIDN'T THINK HE'D BE THIS PATHETIC.

...CLOVER?!

A FOUR-LEAF......

H-HEY...

FOUR-LEAF... FROM THE LEGEND?

I'LL BECOME...

THE FIRST WIZARD KING ALSO RECEIVED ONE.

IT SUPPOSEDLY HAS GREAT POWER.

...THE WIZARD KING.

...

THAT GRIMOIRE HAS *GOOD FORTUNE* WITHIN IT, RIGHT?!

HE GOT THAT GRIMOIRE?

WHOA
...

THAT'S AWE-SOME!

WHOOAAAA!

WOOOOOH

THIS HAS GOT TO BE A MISTAKE!

BUT HE'S JUST A POOR ORPHAN!

YOU'RE AMAZ-ING!

HE'S THE RAY OF HOPE OF THIS REGION!

YUNO!

OOOOH

YOU'RE SO COOL, YUNO!

THERE'S NO WAY!

TMP

ALL RIGHT! LET'S HEAD HOME AND PREPARE FOR THE FEAST!

WOOH

ASTA...

IS HE OKAY?

I didn't think something so great...

...would appear in this backwater town.

HEH? HEH? HEH?

...BUT I DIDN'T KNOW IT WAS SO BAD THAT I WOULDN'T GET A GRIMOIRE.

I KNEW I HAD NO SKILL IN MAGIC...

DAZED

"...BECOMES THE WIZARD KING!"

"LET'S SEE WHO..."

I GUESS...

...I CAN'T DO IT.

"IT'S A PROMISE."

NAH. HE PROBABLY DOESN'T EVEN REMEMBER.

THERE'S NO WAY!

YUNO... DID I DISAPPOINT HIM?

LIKE I'M GONNA GIVE UP!

THAT'S...

HM?

I'M GOING TO DO IT! EVEN IF IT TAKES A YEAR, OR EVEN TWO, I'LL WORK HARD UNTIL I GET A GRIMOIRE!

WAIT FOR ME, YUNOOO!

ARRGHHH

BWAHAHAHA, DON'T UNDERRATE ME, DESTINY!

The man of the day shouldn't be staying so late.

...

81

VWOOOOOOSH

IT PREVENTS THE MAGIC AND MOVEMENTS OF THOSE IT CAPTURES!

EMBODI-MENT MAGIC "MAGIC-BINDING IRON CHAIN FORMATION."

...

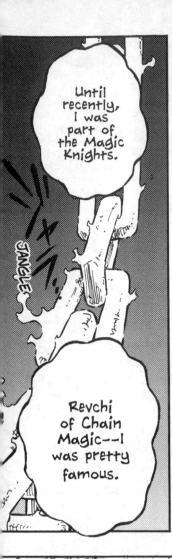

Until recently, I was part of the Magic Knights.

Revchi of Chain Magic--I was pretty famous.

Heh heh heh.

WHO THE HECK...

...ARE YOU?

Only the chosen gets to use his grimoire.

HEH HEH!

But an underworld collector would pay insane money for a four-leaf clover grimoire!

But now I'm just a wretched ol' thief.

I CAN'T POSSIBLY FIGHT HIM WITH JUST PHYSICAL TRAINING.

THUD

SO THIS IS THE POWER OF MAGES OUTSIDE THIS TOWN.

WHAT A HEAVY BLOW!

...

...

Since you worked so hard, I'll tell you something.

These chains tell me the magical powers of those who touch them.

You put up a decent struggle, lad.

HEH HEH HEH!

No wonder you can't use magic at all!

You were probably just born that way.

And you have absolutely no magical powers within you.

WHAT?

THEN NO MATTER HOW HARD I TRY, I CAN'T USE MAGIC?

WHAT THE HECK IS THAT... HEH.

...makes fun of you as well.

I'm sure your friend, the great genius...

Heh heh...

When I think about what you've been through, and what you'll face in the future, I feel pity for you.

I never thought someone like you existed.

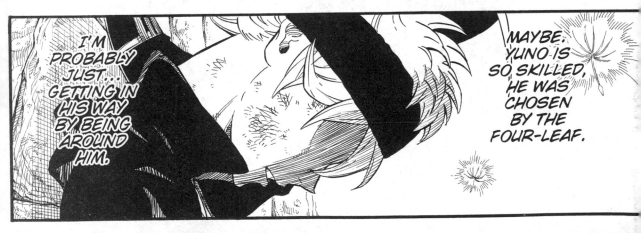

I'M PROBABLY JUST... GETTING IN HIS WAY BY BEING AROUND HIM.

MAYBE, YUNO IS SO SKILLED, HE WAS CHOSEN BY THE FOUR-LEAF.

You were born to be a loser!

You should give up on every- thing.

In this world, you won't be able to do anything. Nothing at all.

I'M NOT DONE YET!

GRRP

GRRP

I'LL...

...KICK THIS GUY'S BUTT!

GRRP GRRP

KLUNK

HOLD ON.

SORRY FOR SHOWING YOU A PATHETIC SIDE OF ME, YUNO.

KLUNK KLUNK

DODGE

What the...?